WHAT

IF YOU

BELIEVED?

31 Beliefs to Act on From
the Living Word to Bring About Life Change

By:

JACKIE DIGHANS

What If You Believed?

31 Beliefs to Act on From
the Living Word to Bring About Life Change

Publisher of Peace

Miles City, Montana

ISBN: 979-8-9877483-1-2

Library of Congress Control Number: 2023902825

Cover and interior design by: worldlight_gfx/fiverr

Editing by: Fine Lines, LLC

Illustrations by: Rayne Idland Photography

All rights reserved by Jackie Dighans and Publisher of Peace.

Printed in the United States of America.

TABLE OF CONTENTS

I want to thank my heavenly Father and the trials that He allowed me to walk through that caused me grow in faith and choose to believe the Word of God over my circumstances. I want to also thank my husband Justin and children (Jayna, Summer, Luke, Logen, Alena, Easton, Jaclyn, Lindy, Blaize, and Evangelia) for being amazing and doing life with me. I am one blessed wife and mom.

INTRODUCTION

What would your life look like if you believed the Word of God? I mean… believed the Word to the extent that it changes everything. What if the Word of God became more real to you than the circumstances in your life?

Start getting in alignment with the Covenant of God one **Belief** at a time.

Take this walk with me through the scriptures and let me show you how each verse can become a part of your life. Let me explain how the scriptures can become alive to you and your situation.

I will give you glimpses of circumstances that I walked through and how God taught me to believe His Word and focus on it rather than all the things that were swirling around me.

The Word is not meant to just make you feel good until the next troubling time comes. It is meant to change your mindset so you can be at peace as the storms of life come and go. It's meant to help you not be moved by the continually changing circumstances but to remain steadfast, standing on the Word, believing the Word. Walking above your circumstances. Standing unmoved in the midst of the trouble.

What if you could find joy in the trials? Not because they are fun or you are denying what is going on, but because you are watching it from your seated place at the right hand of the Father in heaven with Jesus.

"And He raised us up together with Him [when we believed], and seated us with Him in the heavenly places, [because we are] in Christ Jesus." Ephesians 2:6

What if you, Christian, started acting like a believer and started believing the Word? Belief is faith, and when we believe in something we act on it. We act out of our belief. Our belief changes how we see things, what we say, and, finally, what we do. What we believe becomes who we are and how we live.

Are you up for the challenge?

Are you ready to spend some time with me and learn how to believe and apply the Word to your life? Are you ready to transform your life one **Belief** at a time, one verse at a time, one Word of God at a time?

Why wait?

Why live in the mess, the torment, the anxiety, the worry, the sickness, the fear any longer?

Step into life change today, with me right by your side, coaching you. *Covenant Life Coaching* you to come in alignment with the covenant of God so you can experience the full, abundant, best life that He has planned for you. It's time to get rid of the limiting beliefs that are holding you back from running your race and reaching the high call of God.

You won't regret it.

Step into transformation by believing the Word over your circumstances.

The just shall live by faith.

"BUT MY RIGHTEOUS ONE [the one justified by faith] SHALL LIVE BY FAITH [respecting man's relationship to God and trusting Him]; AND IF HE DRAWS BACK [shrinking in fear], MY SOUL HAS NO DELIGHT IN HIM." Hebrews 10:38

We cannot please God without faith. We can't please Him without believing Him, otherwise why do we even bother with God or the Word anyway? It is a waste of time if we don't follow it and the Holy Spirit. We must be determined to follow all of it.

"But without faith it is impossible to [walk with God and] please Him, for whoever comes [near] to God must [necessarily] believe that God exists and that He rewards those who [earnestly and diligently] seek Him." Hebrews 11:6

What would your life look like if you chose to live by faith rather than by everything you see? What if you chose to live by the Word, believing what it says above all the things going on in your life.

"For we walk by faith, not by sight [living our lives in a manner consistent with our confident belief in God's promises]—" 2 Corinthians 5:7

Can you imagine the peace you would have? Can you imagine the stability it would bring to your life?

What if you knew all the things happening good and "bad" were happening for you and your growth as a Christian, as a child of God?

Well friend, it's time to dive into an amazing adventure with the Word of God and walk out in newness. Completely and totally changed by the Word itself—Believe and act on the Living Word.

Your Covenant Life Coach,

Jackie Dighans

BELIEF 1

Deuteronomy 31:8 NLT

"Do not be afraid or discouraged, for the LORD will personally go ahead of you. He will be with you; He will neither fail you nor abandon you."

COVENANT LIFE COACHING

What if you believed...?

... The LORD personally goes before you in your day. Picture it! In your home, He's before you; in your business, God is there; in your job, Jesus is by your side; in your marriage, He's seeing you through; in that relationship, He's giving wisdom. What if you can apply this verse to your children? He personally goes before my children. He knows their every step. He sees their future. He personally goes ahead of _____. You apply this promise to your life where you need it.

Can you picture the Lord going before you personally? I like the word "personally." It makes me feel cared for or watched over. The Lord isn't just sending one of His servants to check on me. He is personally attending to my life. He is personally looking out for me. He watches my steps with His eye. Selah (stop and think of that). He is with me. He will not disappoint me. God will not check out on me in the middle of my life. He won't suddenly fall asleep on me. My heavenly Father will show up. He has already seen my future; He is before me. I will not be left alone. I will not be abandoned. If there is any feeling that I am alone, it's a lie from the enemy. Satan wants me to think God has forsaken me and left me. I will not believe that. It's not true. Either this Word is true, or the Word of God is all a farse. Which will you believe? The Word of God or the other things you are hearing? I will not fear. I will not be discouraged. I will not be afraid. I will not be dismayed, shaken, troubled, disturbed, or distressed. I will not be upset, alarmed, or rattled. I will believe the Word. The truth sets me free. I will live according to the Word and not what I see. The Lord is with me even to the end of the age. Are you ready to believe this?

Heavenly Father, thank You so much for personally going ahead of___. I know You are with___. You will not fail nor abandon___. I will not be afraid nor discouraged. In Jesus' name.

Fill in the blanks with your personal situation and do not waiver from this belief.

It is the LORD who goes before you; He will be with you. He will not fail you or abandon you. Do not fear or be dismayed." Deuteronomy 31:8 AMP

More Meditation: Matthew 28:20

I choose to believe...

_____

_____

_____

_____

_____

_____

_____

_____

_____

_____

_____

_____

_____

_____

_____

_____

_____

_____

_____

_____

_____

BELIEF 2

1 Corinthians 6:19-20 NLT

"Don't you realize that your body is the temple of the Holy Spirit, who lives in you and was given to you by God? You do not belong to yourself, for God bought you with a high price. So you must honor God with your body."

COVENANT LIFE COACHING
What if you believed...?

… You do not belong to yourself. God bought you with a price. How does believing this verse change your life? Are you all about your own agenda, doing what you want in this life? Why? You are not your own property. Stop doing your own thing and start acknowledging God in everything. Why are you living for yourself? You are God's property, purchased with the precious blood of His Son, Jesus. Have you ever thought of asking Him what He wants you to do? Where He wants you to go? What He wants you to wear? What He wants you to say?

You have been made to be His. He has given you Holy Spirit as a gift. He is within you. You have been created to bring God into your world. Don't you want to be in tune with His plan for your life? His ways are good, and they are higher than our ways. We won't always understand His ways, but we can trust Him. Will you trust Him? Will you just sit and soak in the fact that your heavenly Father bought you with a high price? Selah. Wow! You were not cheap. You are worth so much to Him. You have purpose in this life. He sent His Son to die so He could have you and give you life. He saved you because He loves you. Will you honor and glorify God with not only your body and how you treat it, but also glorify Him with your life? You show you love Him by obeying Him. By yielding your life to Him. By following Him. Will you let Him live through you? Will you live as His property? You won't be sorry. I promise. I have experienced laying down my life, dying to myself, giving Him control of me. I didn't like the mess I was making of my life, let alone the anxiety and fear that was building. When I chose to let go of the reigns of my life, it was so freeing. Everything came together better than I could have imagined!

Heavenly Father, thank You so much for the gift of Holy Spirit within me. I know that I do not belong to myself. I know I am Your property because You bought me with the precious blood of Jesus. Thank You for seeing my worth and purchasing me at such a high price. Thank You for choosing me to honor and glorify You with my life. I choose to let go of the reigns today. Help me to believe and walk in the Spirit. In Jesus' name.

> *"Do you not know that your body is a temple of the Holy Spirit who is within you, whom you have [received as a gift] from God, and that you are not your own [property]? You were bought with a price [you were actually purchased with the precious blood of Jesus and made His own]. So then honor and glorify God with your body." 1 Corinthians 6:19-20 AMP*

More Meditation: Acts 20:24

I choose to believe...

_____

_____

_____

_____

_____

_____

_____

_____

_____

_____

_____

_____

_____

_____

_____

_____

_____

_____

_____

_____

_____

_____

Belief 3

Colossians 3:3 NLT

"For you died to this life, and your real life is hidden with Christ in God.

Covenant Life Coaching

What if you believed…?

… You are dead to this life. What if you believed that your new, real life is hidden with Christ in God? As a mom of ten children, I realized I didn't have a life. I mean nothing I wanted to have happen was working out especially with several children in my home. Unless I died to my own agenda, my own ways, my own wants and desires, and chose to pick up His; I would be upset all the time. I would be constantly disappointed. Who wants to live that way? I knew I didn't. This verse became real to me. I died to this life. I hid myself in Christ. One night when my husband was at his lowest point in depression and breakdown, angry, perverse words were spewing out of his mouth. Our tenth child was a baby. I knew the only way I could survive this situation was to live in Christ, hidden in Him. And so that is what I did. I left my natural life and stepped into the supernatural life with Christ. I was already a believer, a Christian, but I wasn't yielded to God until that night. Since then, my life has never been the same. I live in that new, yielded life with Christ in God. Alive to God. Are you ready to leave your old life, to die to this world? And step out into your new life in Christ? Is it working your way? Do you want to continue the way it is going? Drop your plan, perfectionism, your way, etc. It's not worth the anxiety, worry, depression, or constant rollercoaster of emotions to stay in this place. He surrounds you with songs of deliverance. Hiding yourself in Him brings freedom. It brings safety. It brings joy. God has you covered in every way.

Heavenly Father, I choose to let this life go, my agenda, my plans, my perfectionism, and step into life in Christ. I hide myself in You. I die to this world and live in the supernatural. Thank You for being my safe place. My hiding place. In Jesus' name.

"For you died [to this world], and your
[new, real] life is hidden with Christ in God." Colossians 3:3 AMP

More Meditation: Psalm 32:7

I choose to believe...

_____

_____

_____

_____

_____

_____

_____

_____

_____

_____

_____

_____

_____

_____

_____

_____

_____

_____

_____

_____

_____

_____

_____

_____

BELIEF 4

James 1:2-4 NLT

"Dear brothers and sisters, when troubles of any kind come your way, consider it an opportunity for great joy. For you know that when your faith is tested, your endurance has a chance to grow. So let it grow, for when your endurance is fully developed, you will be perfect and complete, needing nothing.

COVENANT LIFE COACHING

What if you believed...?

… You can consider it pure joy when you face trials of many kinds. You may ask, "Why would I do that?" What if it's only because you know the testing of your faith through the trials that come will produce patience in you? I like to just stop at "produce" something in you. Too often we let the trials produce anxiety, depression, bitterness, resentment, and negative thoughts, feelings, and actions so that we spiral down in life rather than grow. Instead, what if we chose patience, endurance, self-control, faithfulness, and positive thoughts, feelings, and actions creating growth, an upward motion? Why waste the trials that come? My thought is that I don't want to have to go through the same thing the same way again. Meaning if I do need to go through a similar trial, I want to go through it stronger, with more faith. What will allow you to make this shift in your mindset to walk through trials differently? It doesn't really matter what the trials are. We all look at them differently, according to what we have been exposed to previously. I like to compare them to storms. They come and go. They are all different severities. Some hit harder than others. We get to decide how we go through them. Storms of life are a part of life. You don't get to decide what types of storms come, but you do get to decide how you go through them. Will you decide to grow through them because they will make you mature and complete, lacking nothing? Wouldn't it be nice to be more mature spiritually for the next trial? Wouldn't it be amazing to be able to offer the wisdom you gained through your life trials to someone in need? Choose growth. Choose to believe.

Heavenly Father, I will choose to consider it pure joy whenever I face trials. I am tired of riding an emotional rollercoaster in life. I am ready to choose growth. I don't want to go through the same thing the same way again. I want my trials to produce patience in me and make me mature and complete, lacking nothing. I believe these storms of life are for me and my spiritual growth. Thank You! In Jesus' name.

"Consider it nothing but joy my brothers and sisters, whenever you fall into various trials. Be assured that the testing of your faith [through experience] produces endurance [leading to spiritual maturity and inner peace]. And let endurance have its perfect result and do a thorough work so that you may be perfect and completely developed [in your faith], lacking in nothing."
James 1:2-4 AMP

More Meditation: Romans 8:28

I choose to believe…

BELIEF 5

Matthew 22:36-38 NLT

"Teacher, which is the most important commandment in the law of Moses?"
Jesus replied, "'You must love the Lord your God with all your heart, all
your soul, and all your mind.' This is the first and greatest commandment."

COVENANT LIFE COACHING

What if you believed…?

… There is a greatest commandment. What if you really believed that this commandment is the most important? What would you do? Would you apply it to your life? Would you search your heart and ask yourself and God, "What does it look like to love the Lord my God with all my heart, with all my soul, and with all my mind?" What would that look like for you to believe this Word? To love God first above all things? Can you put your heart into loving God? Can you put your soul into loving God? Can you put your mind into loving God? I remember when I first got serious about applying this verse to my life. I remember closing my eyes and imagining what it would look like for me to choose to love God with all my being. That looked like worshipping Him with my whole self, with my heart. Not just the act of worship but putting my love toward God and creating a heart of thankfulness. Choosing to be thankful, choosing to love God because of all He has done for me. Creating a heart of thankfulness because He sent His only Son to die in my place. Ponder that and meditate on it. If there is anything in your life that you are putting before God, that you are loving more than Him, it must go—meaning that love for that other person, thing, idea, must not have priority over God in your life. If you really believe that to love the Lord your God with all your heart, with all your soul, and with all your mind is the first and greatest commandment, how will your life look? What changes do you need to make in your life in order to act on this verse? As you do this, the change will be seen by others. Another verse talks about loving the Lord your God with all your might or with all your strength. What does that look like, to love God with all your might and all your strength? I encourage you, friend, to ponder this verse and walk it out in your life.

Heavenly Father, I want to love You with all my heart with all my soul and with all my mind because You tell me in Your Word that this is the first and greatest commandment. I am thankful for all You have done for me. I choose to believe this Word. Show me how, guide me. Help me walk this out daily. In Jesus' name.

"Teacher, which is the greatest commandment in the Law?" And Jesus replied to him, "'YOU SHALL LOVE THE LORD YOUR GOD WITH ALL YOUR HEART, WITH ALL YOUR SOUL, AND WITH ALL YOUR MIND.' This is the first and greatest commandment." Matthew 22:36-38

More Meditation: Deuteronomy 6:5

I choose to believe...

_____

_____

_____

_____

_____

_____

_____

_____

_____

_____

_____

_____

_____

_____

_____

_____

_____

_____

_____

_____

BELIEF 6

Matthew 22:39-40 NLT
"A second is equally important. Love your neighbor as yourself.
The entire law and all the demands of the prophets are based
on these two commandments."

COVENANT LIFE COACHING

What if you believed…?

… Loving your neighbor as you love yourself reveals your love for God. Do you love yourself? I don't mean a vain love of yourself. Do you see the worth and the value that God has put on you? Do you see how special you are to Him? How loved you are? To love your neighbor, in order to love the other person or other people, this requires you to love yourself first. What don't you like about yourself? What don't you love about yourself? Sit and ponder this for just a moment. Did you know that you're created in the image of God? That you're God's workmanship created in Christ Jesus to do good works? Why don't you love yourself? Did something happen in the past? Are you believing words of other people rather than believing God's Word? He calls you His beloved. He's on your side. He's fighting for you. You are already approved. You are already accepted. The question is: Will you accept yourself? Just as you are. Just because God has already accepted you. You are a child of God. You are loved. Once you get that settled with God and receive His love for you, realizing nothing can separate you from His love, you will no longer live in fear. Perfect love casts out all fear. Then and only then can you love yourself and, in turn, love your neighbor. Your neighbor is your husband, your children, your extended family, your friends, and strangers. You can even love your enemies. When fear is cast out, love remains. His love is a gift to you. It's the same love that He has for Jesus. Will you receive it? It's the royal law. It's the greatest commandment. You are worthy, yes, you. Because He said you are.

Heavenly Father. Thank You for showing me this. Thank You for showing me how much You love me. Because of Your love for me, I can see my worth and my value and love myself. It's not easy, God. I know all my faults, all my flaws. Every imperfection. But I will choose to love myself so that I, in turn, can love other people. I know loving myself is a choice. I receive Your love for me. Thank You for helping me walk in love. In Jesus' name.

"The second is like it, you shall love your neighbor as yourself, [that is unselfishly seek the best or higher good for others]. The whole law and the writings of the prophets depend on these two commandments."
Matthew 22:39-40 AMP

More Meditation: John 17:23

I choose to believe…

_____

_____

_____

_____

_____

_____

_____

_____

_____

_____

_____

_____

_____

_____

_____

_____

_____

_____

_____

_____

_____

BELIEF 7

Philippians 4:19 NLT

"And this same God who takes care of me will supply all your needs from his glorious riches which have been given to us in Christ Jesus."

COVENANT LIFE COACHING

What if you believed...?

... God supplies all your needs according to His riches. He liberally supplies every need. Liberally means generously. What if He supplies your needs generously? Will you believe that? The Word says He takes care of you. In my home, raising ten children, I realize that I can't supply all the needs. You can only imagine how many needs there would be in a home with that many children! I remember when I said, "OK, God. I don't know how to make this all work, but what I do know is that I'm going to believe You. I'm not going to look in my checkbook. I'm not going to search the stores. When things come up, when needs come up, I'm going to ask You." So, I did, and I watched God supply every need. He has told me to wait. At times the need may go away. I do not rely on the stores. I do not rely on other sources, like what my checkbook reads. I rely on God first. I go to Him first. Then He leads me on how to take care of that need. What would your life look like if you believed that He will take care of your needs? What if you just walk that way? What if you simply believed? God, this need has come up: my kids need shoes, we need groceries, our car needs fixed, the roof is leaking. What if you simply believe that He will take care of it and walk out asking if there is anything that you need to do? At one point, we had a leak in our roof. I asked God how we were going to take care of it. After we had done all we knew to do, a hailstorm came through. One piece of hail went through our skylight. From this, we ended up getting an entire new roof; the leak was fixed. I could've thought, "This hailstorm is horrible! Now we have a hole in our roof!" But I knew, I believed, that God was going to work it out. I not only got a new roof, but I got a copper metal roof. From that hailstorm, we also got all new garage doors. We have three stalls in our garage, and all of them were replaced. All I can say is, thank You God! You're so faithful! He is faithful. He works things out for our good. You can be discouraged, but why? That's the easy response. Why not choose to believe? He wants to show up for you.

Heavenly Father, thank You so much for your faithfulness. God, I will start believing that You will supply all my needs and all of the needs of my family. That You not only supply, but You supply liberally. You are generous with me. I thank You, Father. I praise You. I expect to see good things coming and You showing up. In Jesus' name.

"And my God will liberally supply (fill until full) your every need according to His riches and glory in Christ Jesus." Philippians 4:19 AMP

More Meditation: Psalm 119:17

I choose to believe...

_____

_____

_____

_____

_____

_____

_____

_____

_____

_____

_____

_____

_____

_____

_____

_____

_____

_____

_____

_____

_____

BELIEF 8

Isaiah 54:17 NLT

"But in that coming day no weapon turned against you will succeed. You will silence every voice raised up to accuse you. These benefits are enjoyed by the servants of the LORD; their vindication will come from Me. I, the LORD, have spoken!"

COVENANT LIFE COACHING

What if you believed…?

… No weapon formed against you shall prosper. Every voice raised up to accuse you will be silenced. It says in the Word that these benefits are enjoyed by the servants of the Lord. Ask yourself, "Am I a servant of the Lord? Am I walking in these benefits?" These benefits are for you. It says peace, righteousness, security, and triumph over opposition is part of your inheritance. One area where I apply the verse, "No weapon formed against me shall prosper", is my health. I was diagnosed with being on the verge of a Grand Mal seizure when I was just pregnant with my tenth baby. I believed, spoke this verse, walked it out, and was healed over a season. I used it again after I had my tenth baby. I got home and realized I had a blood clot in my leg. Again, I spoke out in belief these verses, "No weapon formed against me shall prosper; By your stripes, I am healed." When something comes up against you or your family, your business, your home, what if you believe this verse? What if you believe that whatever comes against you will not succeed? What if you believe it can't overtake you? What if you believe that those words spoken against you will be silenced? Or that you will silence them? How can you silence them? What if it's by not believing them or responding to them? Will you believe these words? Will you believe that the Lord will clear you of any blame or anything spoken against you? Think of all the areas in your life where you can apply this verse and start believing it for your life today.

Heavenly Father, thank You for these benefits in my life. I declare that I have peace, righteousness, security, and triumph over all opposition in my life. I will apply this to sickness and other things that come up against me or my family. I won't pay attention to voices that rise up against me, accusing me. I choose to believe You. In Jesus' name.

"No weapon that is formed against you will succeed; And every tongue that rises against you in judgment you will condemn. This [peace, righteousness, security, and triumph over opposition] is the heritage of the servants of the LORD. And this is their vindication from Me, says the LORD."
Isaiah 54:17 AMP

More Meditation: I Peter 2:24

I choose to believe...

_____

_____

_____

_____

_____

_____

_____

_____

_____

_____

_____

_____

_____

_____

_____

_____

_____

_____

_____

_____

_____

_____

_____

_____

BELIEF 9

Matthew 6:14 NLT

*"If you forgive those who sin against you,
your heavenly Father will forgive you."*

COVENANT LIFE COACHING

What if you believed…?

… If you forgive those who sin against you, you will be forgiven. What if you forgive those who are reckless with you and willfully sin against you? Do you believe that you also will be forgiven? And that if you don't forgive that you won't be forgiven? Not forgiven— is that really the place you want to put yourself? It is a choice to forgive or not to forgive. You may think forgiving is letting someone off the hook. It's letting yourself off the hook—set yourself free! The question is, will you forgive others? Yes, the ones who did that to you. The ones who caused a lot of pain in your life and in the lives of your children and maybe even your spouse. There was a time in my life, and not only one time, but this one that I really remember, when I felt stripped of who I was as a mom and as a wife. It was because of a situation that had happened. I knew that I had to get to the point of setting the other people free so that I could be free. Quickly, I labored to enter rest, forgiveness. I said out loud, "I forgive them" before I was even feeling like I forgave them. I said it and I walked toward it, and I did not allow myself to continue to have negative thoughts toward them. Thoughts came, but I did not entertain them.

Instead, I put together a short prayer for them. Something that I could think about and say whenever the negative thoughts would try to come. I would pray, "Thank you, Lord, that these people are a blessing to others. I do not know why they did the things they did or said the things they said. That's between you and them. Thank you for blessing them. In Jesus' name."

I knew I had a choice of how this played out. I didn't want to stay stuck in bitterness, resentment, and anger. I didn't want to be unforgiven. As hurt as I was and as much as I could not be with these people for a season, I chose to forgive them and to grow through this situation. It set me free. I worked on me. It really had nothing to do with them. We can't change others or control everything that happens. Now, I have a peaceful relationship with them, and it's because I chose to forgive.

Father, help me to forgive. I know forgiveness doesn't mean that I agree with what other people have done. Forgiveness means that I set them free so that I can be free. I allow You to deal with them, Father. I'm not weighed down by unforgiveness in my life. Thank You, Father, for forgiving me as I forgive others. In Jesus' name.

"For if you forgive others their trespasses [their recklessness and willful sins], your heavenly Father will also forgive you." Matthew 6:14 AMP

More Meditation: Colossians 3:13

I choose to believe...

_____

_____

_____

_____

_____

_____

_____

_____

_____

_____

_____

_____

_____

_____

_____

_____

_____

_____

_____

_____

_____

BELIEF 10

Isaiah 53:5 NLT
"But He was pierced for our rebellion, crushed for our sins.
He was beaten so we could be whole. He was whipped so we could be healed."

COVENANT LIFE COACHING

What if you believed…?

… He was pierced for your rebellion. What if you believed that He was crushed for your sins? That He was beaten so you could be made whole? He was whipped so that you could be healed? What if He really was wounded for your transgressions? What if He was crushed for your wickedness, your injustice, your wrongdoing? It was the punishment required for your well-being. It fell on Him. What love the Father has for us! What if you believed that by His stripes you are healed? That's where you come from— already healed. You begin healed in life. When something comes on you, what if you simply ask the Lord, "How are we taking care of this?" What if you don't create all the drama around it? Does it create a thankfulness in your heart to think that God sent His Son for you, for your healing? He died to make you whole. He died a horrible death for your well-being. I don't know about you, but that creates such a thankfulness, such a love for my heavenly Father and for Jesus. That He would be willing to sacrifice His Son, and that Jesus was willing to give His life for me. Like in Romans 5:8, where it talks about while we were still sinners, He died for us. What a kind, loving act toward us! He didn't wait for us to do the right thing. He didn't wait for you to get your life "in order". The sacrifice was made for us even before we said yes to Him. I'm so thankful that He was willing to do that for me and you. I walk in the healing and the wholeness that He died for. I start from a place of "I am healed, and I am whole." That's where we, as Christians, must live from; Jesus died for that. You are healed, whole, and forgiven.

Heavenly Father, thank You so much for dying for me. Thank You for being whipped for me, for being crushed for me. Thank You for taking away my sins. Thank You for making me healed and whole. I want to live that way. God, I want to believe this so much that it changes the way that I live. Nothing broken. Nothing missing. Nothing wrong because You already died and made all things right. In Jesus' name.

"But He was wounded for our transgressions, He was crushed for our wickedness [our sin, our injustice, our wrongdoing]; The punishment [required] for our well-being fell on Him, And by His stripes (wounds) we are healed." Isaiah 53:5 AMP

More Meditation: Romans 5:8

I choose to believe...

_____

_____

_____

_____

_____

_____

_____

_____

_____

_____

_____

_____

_____

_____

_____

_____

_____

_____

_____

_____

_____

_____

_____

BELIEF 11

Romans 6:11 NLT

*"So you also should consider yourselves to be dead
to the power of sin and alive to God through Christ Jesus."*

COVENANT LIFE COACHING

What if you believed...?

... You are dead to sin and alive to God through Christ Jesus. What if you considered yourself and your relation to sin broken? What if you considered yourself alive to God in unbroken fellowship with Him in Christ Jesus? I was in a meeting recently where we were all asked to share our sins. I was sitting there asking God, "What are my sins? Why can't I think of a sin, a specific sin, in my life? I knew it wasn't because I thought I was perfect (because I know I'm not). I just couldn't think of one on the spot like that. I ended up not having to share in the group because of time. I continued to seek God about the situation. What He showed me was this verse that if I consider myself dead to sin and to the power of it but alive to God, then I'm not focusing on my sin. I'm keeping short account with God when I do something wrong. I ask for forgiveness. I change my ways. I turn from my wrong and I move forward. I live alive to God, to the things of God, to the fruits of the Spirit, and to my life with Christ. We must focus more on our life in Christ than we do on sin— we can't focus on both. When we get saved, it tells us in the Word that old things have passed away. All things are new. We must let that old life, the life of sin, die. This allows us to grow, to go toward our life with Christ, and to focus on our life with God and all that being alive to God means. What will your life look like if you consider yourself dead to sin? Dead to the power of sin; alive to God. What will you need to shift in your mindset to become more alive to God today? Start that journey today. God will meet you there.

Heavenly Father, thank You that as I came into a relationship with You, old things passed away. I consider myself dead to sin but alive to God. Thank You that I can now focus on where I'm going rather than where I've been. Thank You that I can live in the fruits of the Spirit. I choose to focus on the power of God in my life rather than the power of sin and death. All things are new in my life in Christ. Today, I live alive to God but dead to sin. In Jesus' name.

"Even so, consider yourselves to be dead to sin [and your relationship to it broken], but alive to God [in unbroken fellowship with Him] in Christ Jesus." Romans 6:11 AMP

More Meditation: 2 Corinthians 5:17

I choose to believe...

_____

_____

_____

_____

_____

_____

_____

_____

_____

_____

_____

_____

_____

_____

_____

_____

_____

_____

_____

_____

_____

_____

_____

BELIEF 12

Ephesians 3:20 NLT
"Now all glory to God, who is able, through his mighty power at work within us, to accomplish infinitely more than we might ask or think."

COVENANT LIFE COACHING

What if you believed…?

… Through His power at work in us, He is able to accomplish infinitely more than we ask or think. He is able to carry out His purpose and do superabundantly more than all that we dare ask or think, and infinitely beyond our greatest prayers, hopes, or dreams. What if you believed that? What if He could do more in your life? I remember the days as I was raising my children. I needed God to do more. Sibling rivalry was at a high point. My husband and I were struggling in our marriage. I needed God to do more in our home as far as helping it to run more efficiently. I just needed Him to show up in my life supernaturally. I asked Him to, and I believed that He would. I saw Him help me with my children, with our home, with my marriage, with our business. Just all the areas. I watched Him show up. What would your life look like if you believed that He could do more than you ask? What are you asking? What if He can do more than that? What are you dreaming? Will you believe that He can do superabundantly more than what you're dreaming, praying, thinking, and believing? Wow! That blows my mind. God is so good. He moves beyond our limited minds. His ways are higher than ours. His thoughts are higher than ours. He has your best in mind. He's looking out for us. He'll do more than we could even think to ask Him, even just in our daily lives. Selah, pause and think of that.

Heavenly Father, I need You to do more in my life. I need You to show up supernaturally with my children, in my home, for my marriage. Thank You that You do more than imaginable. I know You will do that if I believe You will. I choose to believe You. I thank You that You are working things out for my good. Doing more than my limited mind could even pray, hope, or dream. In Jesus' name.

"Now to Him who is able to [carry out His purpose and] do superabundantly more than all that we dare ask or think [infinitely beyond our greatest prayers, hopes, or dreams], according to His power that is at work within us," Ephesians 3:20 AMP

More Meditation: Isaiah 55:8-9

I choose to believe...

_____

_____

_____

_____

_____

_____

_____

_____

_____

_____

_____

_____

_____

_____

_____

_____

_____

_____

_____

_____

_____

_____

_____

_____

BELIEF 13

Psalm 23:1 NLT

"The LORD is my shepherd; I have all that I need."

COVENANT LIFE COACHING

What if you believed…?

… The Lord is your shepherd to feed, to guide, and to shield you. He feeds you both physically and spiritually. He guides your way. He shields you from all harm. You are protected. He's your shepherd. He watches over your every need. How differently would you live if you acted on this belief? Then the second part of this verse is: What if you believe that you have all you need to the point of not wanting? What if you're thinking, "I want this!" I want a new water bottle; I want a new car; I want a boyfriend/girlfriend, or a spouse? What if you stopped yourself instead and left that place of want? What if you believed that you have all you need rather than being in that constant place of want, which is a place of pressure and struggle? Do you feel that struggle when you're wanting? What if you just rested in the thought that you have all you need? Wanting is not an option in your life. If you have a need or desire that comes up, what if you can just ask God about it, knowing that He will provide at the right time, change your desire, or take the desire from you? He tells us that He supplies every need. You don't have to be in this place of want. Does that make sense? When a desire comes, what if you just ask God about it? You have the Shepherd Who's taking care of you. Ask

Him, believing. Walk with Him. The Lord is your shepherd, you shall not want. What if you believe that and your belief causes you to act on it? What would your life look like? What are you wanting right now? Ask God and then believe that you have all that you need and any desire that comes, He will take care of it. He will bring it about, if it's for you.

Heavenly Father, thank You that You are my shepherd to feed, guide, and shield me. You are my protector. You take care of me. You feed me physically and spiritually. You guide my path. I am not going to be in a place of want anymore. I know that You supply every need. And I believe You for that. If a desire comes up, Father, I'm just going to ask You. I'm not going to stand in a place of pressure to get something. Thank You, Father, for being so good. In Jesus' name.

> *"A Psalm of David. The LORD is my Shepherd [to feed, to guide and to shield me], I shall not want." Psalm 23:1*

More Meditation: John 10:11

I choose to believe...

_____

_____

_____

_____

_____

_____

_____

_____

_____

_____

_____

_____

_____

_____

_____

_____

_____

_____

_____

_____

_____

BELIEF 14

James 4:8 NLT

"Come close to God, and God will come close to you. Wash your hands, you sinners. Purify your hearts, for your loyalty is divided between God and the world."

COVENANT LIFE COACHING

What if you believed…?

… If you come close to God, He will come close to you. What if that is true? Draw near to God with a contrite heart; He will draw near to you. It's like He meets you right there as you are drawing near. He draws near. Sometimes it can feel like it takes a long time, or it is a long road to get to God or feel near to Him. But what if it doesn't take that long because He also comes to you as you go toward Him? What if the key is believing that this verse is true? Try it. I remember when I started coming close to God, He came close to me. He met me there as I sought Him with all my heart, with all my soul, and with all my strength. I believed and imagined God being close to me. What if you wash your hands? What if you come clean of the wrong things that you're doing? What if you purify your heart? What if you forgive and stop looking at things that are wrong or bad. Stop saying things that are negative. Turn from things that bring impurity into your life. Stop judging and stop being jealous, and just love people. What would that look like for you? I like some of the words in this verse, "purifying your unfaithful hearts, you double minded people."

What if you are single minded? What if you follow God and only Him? What if we have hearts of love and things aren't so complicated when we do that? What if we let go of all the darkness, the things that are keeping us from God? What if you are not divided anymore? What if you are fully seeking after and following God? What would your life look like if you believed that these verses are the true words of God? Applying them to your life, you will be changed. Words from God are here to help you in your life. Start believing, fellow Christian, and watch God come near to you as you become single minded and go toward Him.

Thank You, Heavenly Father, that when I draw near to You, You are drawing near to me at the same time. Father, You're helping me wash my hands of the wrong things in my life. You are helping me purify my heart by getting rid of anything that would contaminate my life in any way. Help me to stop being double minded, having one foot in the world and one foot with God. Help me to be single minded, walking toward You with a pure heart. In Jesus' name.

> *"Come close to God [with a contrite heart] and He will come close to you. Wash your hands, you sinners; and purify your [unfaithful] hearts, you double-minded [people]." James 4:8 AMP*

More Meditation: Hebrews 10:22

I choose to believe...

_____

_____

_____

_____

_____

_____

_____

_____

_____

_____

_____

_____

_____

_____

_____

_____

_____

_____

_____

_____

_____

BELIEF 15

Mark 16:17 NLT

"These miraculous signs will accompany those who believe: they will cast out demons in my name, and they will speak in new languages."

COVENANT LIFE COACHING

What if you believed...?

… Miraculous signs accompany you because you believe in His name. In the name of Jesus, because you believe that there is power in His name, you have authority in Christ to cast out demons. Miraculous signs will follow you. You have power and authority given to you because of Who is in you. You will also speak in new languages or tongues because you believe. Obviously, there is a difference between someone who says they believe but who doesn't have any of these signs following them. Where are you? Do you believe only so far and then stop there? Are you limiting God and yourself as a child of God? These miraculous signs WILL follow you as a believer if you believe they will. The thought here is "act like a believer". It should be obvious to others that you are a believer because of what follows you, because of what they see. They will SEE your salvation. Are you walking differently than the world? Are you living differently than the unbelievers? Are you walking in the power and the authority that God has given you? It's a gift you don't have to do anything to earn except to walk in it and receive it as a believer. With a word, you can cast out demons. You know how you have been uncertain about the thought of speaking in tongues? Well, Believer, that's for you also. Look it up. Maybe you've never been taught the truth about it. That's OK. You can look it up for yourself and you can choose to believe and walk in it. Choose today to let the signs follow you.

Heavenly Father, I want to walk in the power and the authority that You have given me. I know this requires me to believe. These miraculous signs will follow me. I will cast out demons in Your name. I will speak in tongues because that's evidence that I have been filled with the Spirit. Thank You, Father, for these amazing gifts, signs, and opportunities that I can walk in. I will be faithful because You are faithful. In Jesus' name.

"These signs will accompany those who have believed: in My name they will cast out demons they will speak in new tongues;" Mark 16:17 AMP

More Meditation: 1 Corinthians 14:2

I choose to believe...

_____

_____

_____

_____

_____

_____

_____

_____

_____

_____

_____

_____

_____

_____

_____

_____

_____

_____

_____

_____

_____

BELIEF 16

Mark 16:18 NLT

"They will be able to handle snakes with safety, and if they drink anything poisonous, it won't hurt them. They will be able to place their hands on the sick, and they will be healed."

COVENANT LIFE COACHING

What if you believed…?

… These signs would follow you. You would be able to handle snakes with safety, to pick up serpents. Does that mean actual serpents or snakes? It could, if you would ever run into such a situation, but, more generally, it means if you handle something that could be dangerous for you and your family unknowingly. What if you were unaware of the danger or were just in a situation where you were forced to do something that could potentially be harmful? Would you be able to believe that you're safe? That it's not going to harm you or your loved ones, even if you drank something poisonous, or if you, your animals, or your kids ingested something that was poisonous? I personally stand on this verse when myself or my children have taken medicine or vaccinations that could have a harmful effect on me or them. Will you believe that there is protection in your situation? What if you just know and believe that? It's becoming who you are: safe, protected. That's the idea. Not that you do something foolishly. It's not testing God in some way, which we are not supposed to do, but that receiving protection is a part of being a child of

God. Just believe that you are covered, or that you're surrounded by the Shield of God. What if you believe that you would be able to place your hands on sick people and they would be healed? What if you walked that way? What if you believed that you had the power and the authority to walk in protection and healing? It's for you personally and for you to minister to others. Wouldn't believing this cause you to respond differently to life situations? Would you be able to show up in a different way? If you believe this and walk in it, would people around you be healed because you chose to obey and lay your hands on the sick? Believer, this could change your life and the lives of those around you. Walk in the authority and the power given to you as you believe in the name of Jesus and walk out this verse in your life!

Heavenly Father, thank You for all these miraculous signs that can follow me because I believe in Your name. I can do these things. I declare that I believe. I will see the sick get well. Nothing deadly can harm me or my children. I choose to believe in the power and authority Your name carries. In Jesus' name.

"They will pick up serpents, and if they drink anything deadly, it will not hurt them; they will lay hands on the sick, and they will get well."
Mark 16:18 AMP

More Meditation: Matthew 10:8

I choose to believe...

_____

_____

_____

_____

_____

_____

_____

_____

_____

_____

_____

_____

_____

_____

_____

_____

_____

_____

_____

_____

_____

_____

_____

BELIEF 17

Romans 5:5 NLT

"And this hope will not lead to disappointment. For we know how dearly God loves us, because He has given us the Holy Spirit to fill our hearts with His love."

COVENANT LIFE COACHING

What if you believed…?

… God's promises never disappoint. We will not be disappointed in what God has told us in His promises. What if we believed that God's love has been abundantly poured out in our hearts through the Holy Spirit that is given to us? What if you believed that His love is in your heart as you step into Him? We have the fullness of His love, the abundance of His love, the feeling of His love in our hearts for other people. We must only choose to walk in it. Like you've heard before, love is a choice. What if you believe that you have the love of God poured into your heart? If it's poured, it's not just dripping, it's a continual stream going into your heart. You are poured into by the Holy Spirit. What if you choose to walk as if this is true? That's what I'm seeing—a continual stream of love, a pouring out of love into our hearts. It's for us. It's for us to lavish on others. That's another scriptural image, that His love has been lavished on us, which I picture like being lavished with lotion. You know when your children have too much lotion and they come to you and they say, "Would you like some of this lotion? I have too much on my hands"? At least, that's what our kids would do! They have enough for themselves and enough to share. What if the love that the Holy Spirit is pouring into your heart is like that? When you encounter others, that love is dripping off you. If they are close to you, if they are in your presence, they're going to get some. It's overflowing from you. What if you lived that way? What if you believed that you have that much love to give away, to immerse people in? It's a choice to love. What if you chose to pick up this love and walk in it toward God, toward yourself, and toward others? It's the first and second commandment. It could be important to follow, don't you think?

Heavenly Father, thank You so much for pouring Your love into my heart. Father, I love You so much. I see how much You love me, which allows me to see my worth and to love myself. I recognize that love You've poured into my heart, the love that You've lavished on me, and I share it with others. I live a life of love. I choose to do it. I choose to love. In Jesus' name.

Such hope [in God's promises] never disappoints us, because God's love has been abundantly poured out within our hearts through the Holy Spirit who was given to us." Romans 5:5 AMP

More Meditation: 1 John 3:1

I choose to believe...

_____
_____
_____
_____
_____
_____
_____
_____
_____
_____
_____
_____
_____
_____
_____
_____
_____
_____
_____

BELIEF 18

Psalm 34:8 NLT
"Taste and see that the LORD is good; Oh,
the joys of those who take refuge in Him!"

COVENANT LIFE COACHING

What if you believed...?

... In stepping out and doing the next thing, you will be able to taste and see that the Lord is good. If you do this, you will be able to taste His goodness. God gave me this verse as I was contemplating whether or not to go on a mission trip the summer after my first year of college. I was afraid and uncertain. I went ahead and signed up believing that I would see and taste the goodness of God as I stepped into an unknown place, a place that I wasn't exactly sure of. I felt like God was leading me to go. So, I went with a group for the summer overseas teaching English in the churches in a city in Asia. I learned so much and had so many experiences. I am so thankful I got a taste of His goodness at that time in my life. I encourage you to step into the next thing. He's bidding you come taste and see that He is good in this unfamiliar place. What if you believe that you could taste and see His goodness in this next place that He is leading you to? Oh, the joys of those who take refuge in Him! Will you take refuge, find safety? Find your safe place in Him. In this world, there's no safe place. He is your Refuge. You will find joy there, and you are blessed and fortunate and prosperous there. You are favored in

Christ. You who take refuge in Him, trust in Him. Believe Him and walk with Him. You will be overflowing with joy. I'm telling you; you won't be disappointed. He's so good. Will you choose to be the one who finds your safe place in God and be blessed, fortunate, prosperous, and favored by God? Start this journey in God's goodness today.

Heavenly Father, thank You so much for bidding me to step into that place where I can taste and see that You are good. It's in a relationship with You. I don't want to be afraid to do the unfamiliar thing. I will walk with You. I choose to believe and walk in Your goodness. I know I will find joy as I take refuge in You. I'm believing You are my safe place. It's nothing of this world. It's in Christ where I find my security and my safety. Thank You for being so good. In Jesus' name.

"O taste and see that the LORD [our God] is good; How blessed [fortunate, prosperous, and favored by God] is the man who takes refuge in Him."
Psalm 34:8 AMP

More Meditation: Psalm 27:13

I choose to believe...

_____

_____

_____

_____

_____

_____

_____

_____

_____

_____

_____

_____

_____

_____

_____

_____

_____

_____

_____

_____

_____

_____

_____

_____

_____

BELIEF 19

Psalm 65:11 NLT

"You crowned the year with a bountiful harvest;
even the hard pathways overflow with abundance."

COVENANT LIFE COACHING

What if you believed...?

... The Lord has crowned this year with a bountiful harvest. In another version, the scripture declares, "He has crowned this year with goodness." It doesn't matter what your year is looking like. What if your focus is on it being a good year, that God has made this year abundant and bountiful in your life, in your family, in your marriage, in your business, etc.? If you look for the goodness and bounty in this year, don't you think you will see it? If you look for the trouble in the year, you will find that. Don't focus on lack. Focus on what God is doing. He has crowned this year with goodness! Crowned means completed or having put the finishing touches on something. What if you believe that He's done that to your year? What if you believe that you are on the path that overflows with abundance? Even hard pathways can overflow with abundance. In another version of scripture, it talks about how your paths drip with abundance. Can you picture the path that you're on as the path of righteousness, the path that the Lord has put you on, and one that is dripping with abundance? This path is increasing with beautiful relationships, a peaceful home, and financial freedom. Everything about your marriage can be made abundant. There is abundance financially and spiritually. Everything is overflowing in your life, it's increasing, and it's beautiful. Superabundance. What would your life look like if you believed this rather than looking at lack, at what is not enough, or at what's not working out? What if you made peace with where you're at and the path you're on? What if you shifted your mindset and believed this verse for yourself? The Lord gave me this verse one year when we were in tight financial times. I grabbed hold of it and believed it as a Word from God. Many times, we believe, oh, that part of the Bible isn't for me, or this isn't what God means there, but what if we simply believe the Word? Start taking it literally. Receive it exactly as you are reading it as you seek Him. Let's not overcomplicate it. You, friend, are on the path that is dripping with abundance. He has crowned your year with His goodness.

Heavenly Father, I love You. Thank You so much for the amazing paths that You have for Your people. Thank You that Your path is abundant. It's overflowing. It's superabundant, bountiful, large, and full. Thank You that every year as children of God is a year that's crowned with Your goodness. And that's where I'm going to walk from now on; I'm going to believe this Word for my life. In Jesus' name.

"You crown the year with Your bounty and Your path overflows."
Psalm 65:11 AMP

More Meditation: Psalm 119:17

I choose to believe...

_____

_____

_____

_____

_____

_____

_____

_____

_____

_____

_____

_____

_____

_____

_____

_____

_____

_____

_____

_____

_____

_____

BELIEF 20

Exodus 14:29 NLT

"But the people of Israel had walked through the middle of the sea on dry ground, as the water stood up like a wall upon both sides."

COVENANT LIFE COACHING

What if you believed...?

… You are like an Israelite. It's a picture of who you are, God's child. That's who we are. What if you believed that in those days, they walked through the middle of the sea on dry ground with walls of water standing up on both sides? It's a picture of us walking through life. How many times have we been in a place where we feel stuck? The road before us is blocked and behind us is pressure. Pharaoh's army was in pursuit from the back. There was no way out for the Israelites. Have you been there my friend, where there was no natural way out? Like when you have a bill come in and you have no way to pay it? There's pressure from behind because you know, there are more bills coming. It creates this space where you can lean on God and watch Him open the way for you. That's what trials are for. They give us a chance to watch God come through. What if you believed that God is going to part the waters for you and you're going to walk across on dry ground? As you put your faith in Him, as you trust Him, you will see the waters part for you. As you walk across, you will not be sinking in the muck. You will be walking, even running, on dry ground. There will not be a struggle through. Can you picture your situation through this lens? He wants to part the water for you in your situation. He wants to make a way for you. He is the God Who Never Changes. He will do the same for you— will you believe? I remember the day the Lord showed me this verse. I needed Him to show up for me like He did in the days of Moses. I asked Him to. What is stopping you from asking? Sometimes we stop the move of God by doubting. It's the Living Word. Why not believe it? Why not live it? Why not act on it?

Heavenly Father, I believe that You are the God Who Never Changes. You are the same yesterday, today, and forever. That's what we've been taught for years. I'm going to start believing that the ways You showed up in the Old Testament can be the same way You show up for me today. I believe that You're going to part the waters in my situation, and I'm going to walk through on dry ground. In Jesus' name.

"But the Israelites walked on dry land in the middle of the sea, and the waters formed a wall to them on their right hand and on their left."
Exodus 14:29 AMP

More Meditation: Hebrews 13:8

I choose to believe...

_____

_____

_____

_____

_____

_____

_____

_____

_____

_____

_____

_____

_____

_____

_____

_____

_____

_____

_____

_____

_____

_____

_____

BELIEF 21

1 John 3:1

"See how very much our Father loves us, for He calls us His children, and that is what we are! But the people who belong to this world don't recognize that we are God's children because they don't know Him."

COVENANT LIFE COACHING

What if you believed...?

... You are God's child. He loves you so much. He's shown you this incredible quality of love. You have been permitted to be named, called, and counted a child of God. That's who you are. Love is the royal law the Kingdom of God. We are children of the High King of heaven. Christian, do you realize that you can walk as royalty on this earth? Our command is to love God, to love ourselves, and to love other people. What if you believed that you are royalty and you're a child of the High King of heaven? He's given you an assignment in His Kingdom here on earth. You must submit to God as you walk in your purpose. This is the way we serve others and build the Kingdom of God. And are you surprised, my friend, the people that belong to the world don't recognize you as a child of God because they don't know Him? When people don't understand you or go against you, they are really going against Him. We are here to represent Him, to be an ambassador for Him. We are here to point people to God and enjoy all the benefits we have in Christ. They will know us by our love. This love has been lavished on us. Another version of scripture says, "He has bestowed His love upon us." He has given it to us as a gift. He has given us the right to this amazing love. What manner of love is it? The incredible kind, the unconditional kind, the kind with no strings attached. This is the love that is a gift. Will you receive this love and give it to others? That's how they'll know us, by our love. What if you believed that you have this love? It's the same love that the Father has for Jesus. Now it's given to us. The Father loves us so much. Receive His love for yourself. Love yourself. In that choice to love yourself, you can love other people. Wow! What a privilege to be named a child of God, to be part of His family and a part of His Kingdom. Let's walk in the royal law of love. Stop being offended. Stop being afraid. Nothing separates you from His love. Be ruled by love, my friend. Don't be angry. Don't be jealous. Don't be bitter. Don't be resentful. Love—it's who you are. It's in you because He's in you.

Heavenly Father, I see this love that You've bestowed on me. Thank You for loving me. Thank You for allowing me to be called Your child. I know that I've been lavished in this amazing love. That's how they'll know I'm Yours. And it's okay if they don't recognize me as a child of God. I'll love anyway. They didn't recognize You either, Jesus. But You still walked in love. And I'm going to do the same. Thank You. In Jesus' name.

"See what an incredible quality of love the Father has shown to us, that we would [be permitted to] be named and called and counted the children of God! And so we are! For this reason, the world does not know us, because it did not know Him." 1 John 3:1 AMP

More Meditation: John 13:35

I choose to believe...

_____

_____

_____

_____

_____

_____

_____

_____

_____

_____

_____

_____

_____

_____

_____

_____

_____

_____

_____

_____

_____

_____

_____

_____

BELIEF 22

Hebrews 12:1 NLT

"Therefore, since we are surrounded by such a huge crowd of witnesses to the life of faith, let us strip off every weight that slows us down, especially the sin that so easily trips us up. And let us run with endurance the race God has set before us."

COVENANT LIFE COACHING
What if you believed…?

… You are surrounded by a cloud of witnesses watching you walk out your life of faith. What are they seeing? They are cheering you on. They want to see you win. The witnesses are in heaven, watching, witnessing the events on earth. Knowing this, will you strip off every weight that is slowing you down? Will you strip off every weight and sin that is entangling you so you can run your race? What's tripping you up? What's holding you back? My friend, let's run with endurance. Let's not quit when it gets hard. Let's push through as we see God and the opportunities before us. Keep going in following and obeying Him. We've got this race set before us. What is the race that you're running? Are you running from something? Are you running toward things? Who are you running toward? It needs to be God, my friend, if you want to succeed. He's got plans for you. Plans to prosper you. Plans to give you a hope and a future. He's on your side. He's fighting for you. He is with you. He's your help. He's your strength. He's your peace and your joy. He is your salvation. Do you believe this? Keep running, my friend. Are there any more weights that are keeping you from moving forward? If so, throw them off. Strip yourselves of them and put on Christ. We are to put off the old ways. They are dead. I remember when God showed me that if the old ways are dead and I'm still doing them, it's like I'm carrying around a dead body. Can you picture that? Carrying a dead body over your shoulder. It's weighty. It's hard. It's heavy. It smells. We are to have the aroma of Christ. If you are carrying around this dead body, then things in your life are going to be rotten. That's why you've got those ugly things coming out of our mouth. Put off the old, it's dead. Live alive to God today. Run your race. Throw off the weights and sin that are holding you back. That are weighing you down. Keep running with God. Toward Him. It's in the pursuit of Him that we win in life.

Heavenly Father, thank You so much for showing me what is weighing me down. Thank You for showing me the sin that is entangling me. I choose to throw those things off today. I choose to lay them aside. I choose to put off the dead man. I put on Christ today. I choose to run my race with and toward You. In Jesus' name.

> *"Therefore, since we are surrounded by so great a cloud of witnesses [who by faith have testified to the truth of God's absolute faithfulness] stripping off every unnecessary weight and the sin which so easily and cleverly entangles us, let us run with endurance and active persistence the race that is set before us."*
> *Hebrews 12:1 AMP*

More Meditation: Ephesians 4:22-24

I choose to believe...

BELIEF 23

Hebrews 12:2 NLT

"We do this by keeping our eyes on Jesus, the champion who initiates and perfects our faith. Because of the joy awaiting Him, He endured the cross, disregarding its shame. Now He is seated in the place of honor beside God's throne."

COVENANT LIFE COACHING
What if you believed…?

… Looking away from all that distracts you and focusing your eyes on Jesus, Who is the Author and Perfecter of your faith, will help you run your race well. He's the champion Who initiates and perfects your faith. We keep our eyes on Him and He helps bring our faith to maturity. He went toward the joy awaiting Him. He chose to endure the cross because of the goal. This goal was to give us life and life more abundant. This brought Him joy. He disregarded the shame of the journey. He didn't pay attention to the difficulty of it. He kept his eyes focused forward. He is now seated at the right hand of the throne of God in the place of honor. The question is, friend, "will you endure the trials, the difficult seasons?" Will you turn away from the things that are trying to distract you from walking out your purpose? Will you instead choose to keep your eyes focused on Jesus? The Word tells us not to look to the right or to the left, but straight ahead. Will you do that? Quit being distracted by all the circumstances, all the comments, anything coming against you. The things that want to stop you from the ultimate joy. This joy is resting in the finished work of the Savior. If you choose to not be distracted and keep your eyes on Jesus, you can sit in those heavenly places. Ephesians tells us that we have been raised with Him and seated with Him in the heavenly places in Christ Jesus. Now while you're living here on earth you can live from that spot as a child of God. Will you endure this road? Will you trust your Savior who has already walked the difficult road? He conquered death. There is nothing for you to fear. There's joy now and ahead as we obey God and walk with Him. You will see the goodness of God.

Heavenly Father, I choose to keep my eyes on Jesus, the Author and Perfecter of my faith. I thank You, Jesus, for enduring the cross and disregarding its shame. I also choose to carry my cross, endure the trials, and disregard any shame, imitating Jesus. I know that there is joy now and ahead as I live this life. I choose to sit down in the heavenly places in Christ as I walk this life out with God. In Jesus' name.

"[looking away from all that will distract us and] focusing our eyes on Jesus, who is the Author and Perfecter of faith, [the first incentive for our belief and the One who brings our faith to maturity], who for the joy [of accomplishing the goal] set before Him endured the cross, disregarding the shame, and sat down at the right hand of the throne of God [revealing His deity, His authority, and the completion of His work]." Hebrews 12:2 AMP

More Meditation: Proverbs 4:25

I choose to believe...

_____
_____
_____
_____
_____
_____
_____
_____
_____
_____
_____
_____
_____
_____
_____
_____
_____
_____
_____
_____
_____
_____
_____
_____
_____

BELIEF 24

Hebrews 12:3 NLT
"Think of all the hostility He endured from sinful people;
then you won't become weary and give up."

COVENANT LIFE COACHING

What if you believed...?

... He endured horrible hostility from sinful people. He was beaten; He was scourged. He was not recognizable after the soldiers were done with Him. He was denied by those that He thought were His friends. He was rejected. He was hung upon the cross. His clothes were gambled for, made into a game. He was laughed at, mocked, and ridiculed. Yet He was innocent. This was done by religious leaders. Those who were head of the church. They prayed the best prayers; they knew the scriptures, but it was only head knowledge. The message had not reached their heart. I remember the time when our family first endured persecution from a religious group. We had left a church peacefully to pursue spiritual growth after we had seen the Lord heal members of our family miraculously. We brought it to the attention of the church leaders. It was apparent that they weren't interested in believing what we had experienced and seen in the Word of God. We switched over to a spirit-filled church that lined up with what God was showing us. Members and friends from our previous church avoided us, others wrote letters of concern, still others came to our house and debated with us. Not one set of friends from the previous church continued the friendship. They treated us like strangers, acting almost afraid of us. Why would this happen, you ask? Religion is legalistic; it doesn't like the freedom we have in Christ. Why wouldn't we be rejected/persecuted for our faith? We hadn't experienced this prior to being filled with the spirit with evidence of speaking in tongues. Religion is judgmental, it's afraid, it wants to build its own; it's uncomfortable with the ways of God. As you walk through trials and difficult seasons, as you walk through rejection by your church or friends because you are following God, remember what Jesus went through for you. This will help you not to become weary and give up. Compared to what Jesus went through, what you are going through— you can endure. He did it for you so you could have life. Are you willing to give your life to Him? You are not living your own life. He is living through you. That's what allows you to endure the path you are on. Keep standing, my friend. Your Savior did it for you, and He's with you. He's fighting for you now. He's on your side now. Keep enduring. The picture is much bigger, and the purpose is much greater than what we see.

Heavenly Father, I see what Jesus endured for me so that I could have life. I know that my life is hidden in Him. It's not my own. I choose to endure the trials and tribulations that come because He is with me. He's my help. It's for a much greater purpose than what I see. Thank You, for being with me and for Your Holy Spirit in me. In Jesus' name.

"Just consider and meditate on Him who endured from sinners such bitter hostility against Himself [consider it all in comparison with your trials] so that you will not grow weary and lose heart." Hebrews 12:3 AMP

More Meditation: Isaiah 52:14

I choose to believe...

BELIEF 25

1 Kings 3:9 NLT

"Give me an understanding heart so that I can govern Your people well and know the difference between right and wrong. For who by himself is able to govern this great people of Yours?"

COVENANT LIFE COACHING

What if you believed…?

… You can ask God to give you an understanding heart, so that you can govern His people well and know the difference between right and wrong. What if this can be true of you? In my story, I asked God to give me an understanding mind and a hearing heart so that I could judge His people well. I was raising my family, I may have had five or six kids, when this verse jumped out at me. I needed God's help discerning good and evil with my children. I believed God would help me; I saw that my children were His people with great purpose in life. I asked God for this understanding and to do this in my heart and in my life so that I could raise these children well. I knew it was an important job that He had given me. I wanted to do my job well. I had been through a season where my sister had passed away from cancer and left three children. I was thankful to have life, to be able to be a mom, to be able to parent my children. My thought was, "I get to live." Knowing God had chosen me to raise these children, I wanted to do it with Him, with His wisdom, with His guidance. He knows what they need. He knows the plan for their life. You could apply this to your business and your employees. As a believer, you are a leader, whether you're in a specific position of leadership or not. You have been chosen. Many are called, but few choose the conditions required to be chosen. You have been called to lead because of Who is in you. Apply this verse where you need it for the position God has given you. Rise up!

Heavenly Father, thank You so much for Your Word and that we can apply it to our lives today. Even though this was a scripture from the Old Testament, a prayer that Solomon prayed, I thank You God, for the understanding mind and hearing heart to judge Your people well. I will learn to discern between right and wrong, good and evil. I walk in this world as a leader. You are in me, and You've created me for this purpose, for such a time as this. In Jesus' name.

"So give Your servant an understanding mind and a hearing heart [with which] to judge Your people, so that I may discern between good and evil. For who is able to judge and rule this great people of Yours?" 1 Kings 3:9 AMP

More Meditation: Proverbs 22:6

I choose to believe...

_____
_____
_____
_____
_____
_____
_____
_____
_____
_____
_____
_____
_____
_____
_____
_____
_____
_____
_____
_____
_____
_____
_____

BELIEF 26

John 6:28-29 NLT

*"They replied, "We want to perform God's works, too. What should we do?"
Jesus told them, "This is the only work God wants from you: Believe in
the one He has sent."*

COVENANT LIFE COACHING

What if you believed...?

...To do the work of God is to believe in the One He has sent. The work
of God is to adhere to, trust in, rely on, and have faith in the One He
sent. The One He sent is Jesus. Jesus is the Word. And He also sent the
Holy Spirit. What our work as believers is to believe! I remember the
days, as a wife and mom, growing our large family; it seemed there was
no end to the needs at home, in the church, in our business, and in
serving others. I asked the Lord what my work was as a Christian. I
needed to know what to say yes to. He brought me to this verse. He
made it very clear and simple and showed me my work is to believe. So,
I started believing the Word. I started believing what it said, and I started
doing what it said. Out of my belief, I acted. I would stop, I would slow
down, and I would listen. I paused and acknowledged God in all my
ways. He began making my path straight. Instead of leaning on my own
understanding, in all my ways, I started acknowledging Him. He showed
me what to do. Life became simpler. I knew what He wanted me to do.
Rather than being confused that I had to do it all or that one thing was

better than the other, I knew to act on what the Word was saying and ask the Holy Spirit. I would do what I felt I was being led to do. What would it look like for you to go to the next level in your walk as a Christian and believe the Word to the point that it changes your life? It is so freeing. We can stop the mind games and all the figuring out and simply believe and obey. Follow Jesus. Walk in the Spirit. Live by the Spirit.

Heavenly Father, thank You so much for this simple act of obedience— to believe. It's childlike. Thank You that it's not hard, but it's as simple as letting go of my own way and doing it Your way in faith. I confess right now that I will do the work You've called me to do. That work is to believe Your Word and to believe the Holy Spirit that You have given me. In Jesus' name.

"Then they asked Him, 'What are we to do, so that we may habitually be doing the works of God?' Jesus answered, 'This is the work of God: that you believe [adhere to, trust in, rely on, and have faith] in the One whom He has sent.'" John 6:28-29 AMP

More Meditation: Proverbs 3:5-6

I choose to believe...

_____
_____
_____
_____
_____
_____
_____
_____
_____
_____
_____
_____
_____
_____
_____
_____
_____
_____
_____
_____
_____
_____
_____
_____

BELIEF 27

Proverbs 18:21 NLT
The tongue can bring death or life; those
who love to talk will reap the consequences."

COVENANT LIFE COACHING

What if you believed…?

…The tongue can bring life or death to you. Those who love to talk will reap the consequences of what they speak, good or bad. What if you believed that those who love life and indulge in speaking of life will eat its fruit? We bear the consequences of the words that come out of our mouths. What if you spoke and talked like you believe that you are either bringing life to your marriage, family, home, or business or death, if you speak negatively? Speak positive words, speak blessing, speak truth. Not just the truth of the facts going on, but the truth of the Word. What if you chose to see and believe what the Word of God says over what your circumstances are saying? Believe that which is beyond or above what's going on around you. Speak the living Word into your life and to those in your circle. Watch it turn whatever it touches around. Watch it change the outcome for good. What if you believed the tongue can bring death? What if what you're saying is keeping life from you and your surroundings? Taking life from your children, your husband; pulling life out of your business. Would you change what you're saying? Would you pause and think more about what you're going to speak? Have you been just letting words fly out of your mouth with no intention or purpose? I remember the day when I realized I needed to be more aware of what I was speaking over my children and my parenting. Instead of speaking that my children were troublemakers, I would say what blessings they were even if they weren't acting like blessings at the moment or even most of the time. Instead of saying, "my husband and I aren't on the same page with training our children", I would say "my husband and I are one and we agree." It is that simple, but a person must be intentional. They must desire something different. It must matter. Speak life. Speak blessing. Speak that which is pure and that which is lovely. Say that which is right, and that which is admirable and excellent and praiseworthy. What if you examine your thoughts on these things? What if your thinking overflows out of your heart and what you are saying flows from what is in your heart? What if it's your heart that speaks? What are you thinking on? What do you have going on in your heart? You can change it by what you're believing.

Heavenly Father, thank You for showing me that what I say matters. I am tired of the mess I have in my life because of what I am speaking over my life. I choose today to pay more attention to what I am saying. I want to speak life into my marriage, home, children, and my business. I know I will see a difference as I speak the living Word over my circumstances. In Jesus' name.

"Death and life are in the power of the tongue, and those who love it and indulge it will eat its fruit and bear the consequences of their words."
Proverbs 18:21 AMP

More Meditation: Philippians 4:8

I choose to believe...

_____

_____

_____

_____

_____

_____

_____

_____

_____

_____

_____

_____

_____

_____

_____

_____

_____

_____

_____

_____

_____

_____

_____

_____

BELIEF 28

Proverbs 18:10 NLT
The name of the LORD is a strong fortress;
the godly run to Him and are safe.

COVENANT LIFE COACHING

What if you believed…?

…The name of the Lord is a strong tower or a strong fortress. If you, the godly, run to Him, run into Him, you are safe. You are set on high and far above evil. A fortress is a heavily protected building— an impenetrable building. What if you speaking the name of the Lord, you being in the name of the Lord, gives you this impenetrable place where you reside? You are in this tower. Any sharp edges, hurt, or pain from circumstances, words, people, or situations cannot harm you. When I was in a very difficult spot in my life, in my marriage specifically, one evening, my husband was in a very negative spot. Negative words were flying out of his mouth. I was at the end of my tenth pregnancy. I knew I couldn't deal with the situation naturally. I pictured myself in the name of Jesus, in my Fortress, my Strong Tower. Wrapped in His love, this Fortress was my safe place. I believed that the name of the Lord, my Fortress, my Strong Tower, was surrounding me. I spoke the name of Jesus in my situation and dwelt there. Anything coming to me— words, situations, trouble, sickness, etc.— first had to go through His Name, my Strong Tower, my Fortress— God. If God is love, then all must go through His love before it reaches you. Any rough edges are softened and made dull as it travels through His love. If trouble can even reach you (remember, the fortress is impenetrable), it is softened and dissolved as it goes through Love. It cannot harm you. You are safe, far above evil. You've been set on high; it cannot reach you. What if you believed this and walked in it? What would your life look like? Dwell in this place. It's amazing. It's in Christ.

Heavenly Father, thank You so much for Your name. Thank You that I can speak it into my life. I can speak it out before me, I can speak it into my situations and circumstances. And it's my safe place. It's a place on high. It's a place where trouble cannot penetrate. Words cannot penetrate. Thank You, Father, for this Strong Tower, for Your name that I can reside in. I choose to live in Your name. In Jesus' name.

"The name of the LORD is a strong tower; The righteous runs to it and is safe and set on high, [far above evil]. Proverbs 18:10 AMP

More Meditation: John 15:9

I choose to believe...

_____

_____

_____

_____

_____

_____

_____

_____

_____

_____

_____

_____

_____

_____

_____

_____

_____

_____

_____

_____

_____

_____

BELIEF 29

Psalm 124:7 NLT
"We escaped like a bird from a hunter's trap.
The trap is broken, and we are free!"

COVENANT LIFE COACHING

What if you believed…?

… When you're feeling trapped, the trap is broken. It may look like you're trapped but it hasn't got a hold on you. The latch is broken. You can step out of this snare. You've escaped just like a bird from a hunter's trap. The bird flies away. You've escaped like a bird. A fowler is one who hunts birds. The hunter is the enemy. The hunter is trying to trap you. His trap is broken. You are free to fly, my friend, like an eagle. What if you can renew your strength? You are not captured. Renew your strength by putting your hope in the Lord. You shall grow wings like eagles. You shall run and not grow weary. You shall walk and not be faint. My friend, step out of the trap. If you feel like you're trapped, what if it's as easy as stepping out? The trap is broken, and the Word says that you have already escaped. What if it takes believing that you're not trapped? The great escape has already happened. Someone else broke the snare for you. Jesus freed you by the shedding of His blood. The scheme of the enemy is to make you think you are stuck. You get to decide what you believe and who you believe in. You can believe the lies of the enemy all your life if you want to. Why not simply believe the truth of the Word of God?

The enemy wants to stop you from doing the next thing in your life. He wants to stop you from seeing your marriage restored, your family unified, and your whole life changed. Step into freedom today. Greater is He Who is in you!

Heavenly Father, thank you so much for showing me that I am free, that this so-called trap doesn't even work. It's broken. It won't latch. There's a hole in it. I can walk out of the snare and that's what I'm choosing to do today. Your Word tells me I have escaped like a bird; I can fly away. I am set free, growing wings like the eagles. I will run and not grow weary. I will walk and not be faint. Thank You for setting me free. You are my Savior. In Jesus' name.

"We have escaped like a bird from the snare of the fowlers; The trap is broken and we have escaped." Psalm 124:7 AMP

More Meditation: Isaiah 40:31

I choose to believe...

_____
_____
_____
_____
_____
_____
_____
_____
_____
_____
_____
_____
_____
_____
_____
_____
_____
_____
_____
_____
_____

BELIEF 30

Joshua 1:8 NLT

"Study this Book of instruction continually. Meditate on it day and night so you will be sure to obey everything written in it. Only then you will prosper and succeed in all you do."

COVENANT LIFE COACHING

What if you believed...?

… Studying this book of instruction continually, reading it, meditating on it day and night and being careful to obey and do everything written in it, will make you prosperous and successful. Have you believed the verse above? If not, how can you start walking it out? What would continually meditating on the Word look like for you? For me, it has looked like going over and over scripture in my mind and with my children. It has looked like speaking it out over my situations and believing it over what I was seeing. We must know and believe the Word before we will obey it. As I walked this verse out in my home, I started putting the Word in my children as I homeschooled them. We often rely on academics to bring prosperity and success. God showed me that meditating on and doing the Word was what brings true prosperity and success. I believed this and made the Word most important. I also made sure that I was doing all I could to be a good example by living the Word before my family and others. Obviously, I am not perfect, but that was my heart's desire. Your actions will line up with your beliefs. Your life will be changed. What could this look like in your life? At one point for me, I read every devotional in my house. It looked like obeying the scriptures I was reading. It meant believing the Word enough for it to change my actions. It meant thinking about the verses and what it would look like for me to do them. It meant instead of believing that the academics would make my children prosper and succeed, that I would be getting the Word in them to help them prosper and succeed in all they do. Will you take the steps you need to today to meditate on the Word day and night so that you will be sure to do everything written in it, not just parts of the Word, but all of the Word? Do you want to prosper and succeed? Then believe this verse. Another scripture tells us, "Blessed is the man who delights in the Word, who meditates on it day and night." What if you woke up thinking about it? What if you went to bed thinking about it? What if you thought about it all day? Like a son said to me one time, "Why do you have to think so biblically all the time?" That made me laugh. Meditating on and delighting in the Word brings blessing and success into your life. Make that your aim today!

Heavenly Father, thank You for Your Word. I'm taking a step to not let this Word depart from my mouth. I choose to meditate on it day and night so that I may be careful to do everything written in it. Doing this will make my way prosperous and successful. I believe that it's only in the meditation and action of Your Word that I am blessed. In Jesus' name.

"This Book of the Law shall not depart from your mouth, but you shall read [and meditate on] it day and night, so that you may be careful to do [everything] in accordance with all that is written in it; for then you will make your way prosperous, and then you will be successful." Joshua 1:8 AMP

More Meditation: Psalm 1:2

I choose to believe...

_____

_____

_____

_____

_____

_____

_____

_____

_____

_____

_____

_____

_____

_____

_____

_____

_____

_____

_____

_____

_____

_____

_____

_____

BELIEF 31

Psalm 63:6-8 NLT

"I lie awake thinking of you, meditating on you through the night.
Because you are my helper, I sing for joy in the shadow of your wings.
I cling to you; your strong right hand holds me securely."

COVENANT LIFE COACHING

What if you believed...?

...He is your helper. What if you chose to cling to Him and believe that His strong right hand holds you securely? His right hand upholds you as you walk through all the ups and downs of life. What you believe is what you will do. What if you believed like the psalmist did? What if you lie awake thinking of God, meditating on the Word through the night? What if you're the psalmist? Picture yourself feeling and living the words of the scriptures. Apply the Word to your life. The Word is an example of what we can be thinking and doing with God. Do you live like He's your helper? It's in knowing He's your helper that you can sing for joy in the shadow of His wings, in the shadow of His protection, like a hen hiding her chicks under her wings. God does this for us. We need to imagine ourselves doing the things the Word shows us. In doing this, the Word comes alive in our lives. Have you allowed Him to help you? Have you chosen to cling to Him as you walk through life? That's when you will see that His right hand is holding you securely. The psalmist has already been through something in his life that has caused him to live out what he is writing here. It's for your benefit, something for you to follow. This is an example for you to live by. It's words to believe from the Living Word. The question is, will you believe this Word and act it out, meditating on God, focusing on Him because He's been your help and protection? Singing for joy, clinging to Him for His right hand has upheld you in your time of need?

Heavenly Father, thank You so much for being my help. I believe I am protected by You. Forgive me for the times I have not run to You. I choose to cling to you. I see that night and day, You have upheld me in my times of need. In my trouble You have been with me. Thank You. In Jesus' name.

"When I remember You on my bed, I meditate and thoughtfully focus on You in the night watches. For you have been my help, and in the shadow of your wings [where I am always protected] I sing for joy. My soul [my life, my very self] clings to You; Your right hand upholds me." Psalm 63:6-8 AMP

More Meditation: Psalm 46:1

I choose to believe...

_____
_____
_____
_____
_____
_____
_____
_____
_____
_____
_____
_____
_____
_____
_____
_____
_____
_____
_____
_____

CONCLUSION

You did it! You went through 31 Beliefs to Act on from the Living Word. Did they change your life? Did you allow them to transform your thinking, your living? There are so many beliefs (scriptures) to act on in the Bible. Keep stepping into more and more.

From this moment forward, view scripture from the thought, "This is for me. What can belief in this do for me and in me? How can I think about my situations differently in light of this truth?"

Allow the Word of God to become more real to you than your physical surroundings. Think on things above, not on things of the earth. Live above the circumstances, not in them. Walk by faith, not by sight. Live in the power and authority that God has given you. Live from on High, standing on the Rock, your Firm Foundation. ACT LIKE A BELIEVER!

You have gotten a taste of what **_Covenant Life Coaching_** looks like in book form. If you would like to work directly with me in group or one-on-one coaching, go to Author Services in the back of this book and contact me. I will give you more details. If you want to get more serious about transformation, then seriously consider coaching with me. See you soon!

Your Covenant Life Coach,

Jackie Dighans

Appendix

I Am a Wife Confession

Jackie Dighans—Your Covenant Life Coach

A wise, understanding, and prudent (sensible, well advised, cautious, far-sighted) wife is from the Lord. Proverbs 19:14

I am a fruitful vine in the heart of our home. Psalm 128:3

The heart of my husband safely and confidently trusts in me and relies on and believes in me securely, so that he has no lack of honest gain or need of dishonest spoil. Proverbs 31:11

I comfort, encourage, and do him only good as long as I have life. Proverbs 31:12

I am an excellent wife, a crown (top or highest part) of my husband. I perfect, complete, and put the finishing touches on him as I walk in Christ. Proverbs 12:4

I am a good thing for my husband, and he obtains favor from the Lord because he has found me a true wife. Proverbs 18:22

I see to it that I respect my husband – I notice him, regard him, honor him, prefer him, appreciate him, venerate or revere him, and esteem, value, prize and favor him. I defer to him, am devoted to him, praise, adore, enjoy, deeply love, and admire him exceedingly. Ephesians 5:33, 1 Peter 3:2

My Amazing
Husband Confession

Jackie Dighans—Your Covenant Life Coach

My husband loves me as Christ loved the church and

gave Himself for her.

He washes me with the Word.

He lives with me in an understanding way.

He nourishes and cherishes me and
loves me as his own

body.

He has left his father and mother and cleaves, is joined,

and sticks to me, his wife.

We are one. Ephesians 5:22–33

My husband is a man/ruler of discernment,

understanding, and knowledge. He is stable.

Proverbs 28:2

My husband refreshes others, and we, too, are refreshed.

He prospers because he is generous. Proverbs 11:25

My husband reverently and worshipfully fears the Lord

and delights in His Word, therefore he is blessed.

My husband is known in the city's gates when he sits
among the elders of the land. Proverbs 31:23

Dighans Family Confession

Jackie Dighans—Your Covenant Life Coach

We reverently and worshipfully fear God, and it is the beginning of wisdom and skill.

We have the mind of Christ, and we can do all things through Him Who gives us strength.

Our work is committed to the Lord, and our plans are established.

Because we obey the Lord, our possessions, and everything we put our hands to, is blessed.

We have been lavished in God's love; therefore, we love each other and others.

We have freedom of utterance. We open our mouths with boldness and courage as we ought in both song and speech, that we may proclaim the mystery of the gospel for which we are ambassadors in chains.

We are joyful when we face trials and temptations because we expect them to produce godliness in us.

We were made for signs and wonders, not destruction.

He is able to do exceedingly, abundantly above all we can imagine
according to the power that is at work in us.

We are delivered from the wicked.

We are taught of the Lord and great
is our peace.

We humble ourselves in the sight of the Lord, and He lifts us up.

I Am a Virtuous
Woman Confession

Jackie Dighans—Your Covenant Life Coach

I am a saintly, upstanding, high-minded, virtuous woman.

I speak wisdom, seek wisdom, walk in wisdom, and listen to wisdom.

I show honor, I am honorable, and I win honor for my husband.

The joy of the Lord is my strength.

I rejoice in the truth. I rejoice in the Lord, and I rejoice in the day.

Kindness is on my tongue.

I fear the Lord, and it is the beginning of wisdom and skill.

I am noble, righteous, and good.

I am a provider, source, and supplier of desirable qualities.

I am industrious, diligent, and hardworking.

I am blessed, and I, in turn, bless others. I am a blessing.

I walk in dignity and am worthy of honor because of Christ in me.

He is My Source Confession

Jackie Dighans—Your Covenant Life Coach

He deals bountifully with me (largely, fully, superabundantly).
Psalm 119:17

He supplies all my needs according to His riches in glory.
Philippians 4:19

God is able to make all grace abound toward me, that I, always having
all sufficiency in all things, may have an abundance for every good
work. 2 Corinthians 9:8

The Lord is my Shepherd [to feed, to guide, and to shield me],
I shall not want. Psalm 23:1

I am debt-free by the miracle power of Jesus.

No more late fees.

No more overdraft fees.

He is my shield and my exceeding great reward. Genesis 15:1

Praying in Tongues or
Praying in the Spirit Confession

Jackie Dighans—Your Covenant Life Coach

Whenever I pray in the spirit, I always pray with faith,

knowing every sound, every syllable,

evokes a powerful response from my Heavenly Father.

I pray unto God and not to man.

I pray out mysteries.

1 Corinthians 14:2

I edified myself.

1 Corinthians 14:4

I build myself up in my most holy faith, praying in the Spirit. Jude 1:20

ABOUT THE AUTHOR

Jackie Dighans is a daughter of God Most High. She has been married to her husband, Justin, for twenty-nine years. Together, they have ten children (yes, they are all biological; no, there are not any twins). The children range from seven to twenty-six years old. They have three married children and four grandchildren. Six children are still in the home, attending public school, and one is single and taking the next steps after graduating, as well as working in the family business. Jackie lives with her family in rural southeastern Montana. Jackie was a homeschool mom for almost twenty years. She attended three years of Bible school and has a certificate in Biblical Studies. Jackie is a Covenant Life Coach. She enjoys speaking at women's events, conferences, retreats, and other services. Jackie helps people come in alignment with the Covenant of God so they can live the full lives He has planned for them. She helps people throw off the weights and sin that entangle them and forget the past so they can run their race and reach the goal of the high call of God. Jackie has authored two other books so far, *COVERED Living in triumph while going through trials*, and *COVERED On A Deeper Level. These books are available on Amazon, Barnes & Noble, as well as other online stores.*

AUTHOR'S SERVICES

As a Covenant Life Coach, Jackie offers one-on-one and group coaching. She also enjoys speaking at retreats, women's events, conferences, and other services.

Contact her at jackiedighans@gmail.com.

You can also find her on Facebook, Instagram, TikTok, and YouTube.

Her podcast, called Dripping with Abundance, is on Spotify.

Jackie's other books are *COVERED Living in triumph while going through trials* and *COVERED On A Deeper Level*. Find them on Amazon, Barnes & Noble, as well as other online stores.

www.ingramcontent.com/pod-product-compliance
Lightning Source LLC
Chambersburg PA
CBHW020317130626
46549CB00003B/903